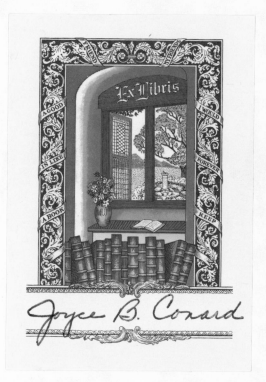

The
FIFTY
STATES
Cookbook

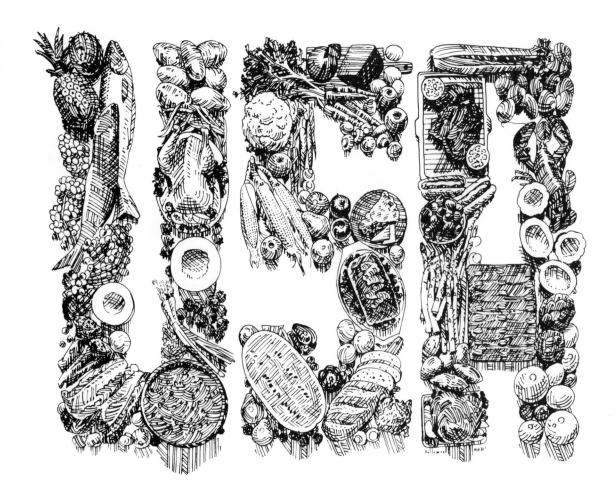

THE FIFTY STATES COOKBOOK

Barbara MacDonald, Carolyn Boisvert, and Peggy Miller:
Contributing Editors

The Culinary Arts Institute Staff:

Helen Geist: Director
Sherrill Corley: Editor • Helen Lehman: Assistant Editor
Edward Finnegan: Executive Editor • Charles Bozett: Art Director
Ethel La Roche: Editorial Assistant • Ivanka Simatic: Recipe Tester
Malinda Miller: Copy Editor • John Mahalek: Art Assembly

Book designed and coordinated by Charles Bozett and Laurel DiGangi

Illustrations by Dev Appleyard

Cover photograph by Zdenek Pivecka

The
FIFTY
STATES
Cookbook

Culinary Arts Institute

1727 South Indiana Avenue, Chicago, Illinois 60616

PHOTO ACKNOWLEDGMENTS

Adolph's Ltd.; Advisory Council for Jams, Jellies and Preserves;
American Dairy Association; American Lamb Council;
American Spice Trade Association; Bob Scott Studios;
California Apricot Advisory Board; California Avocado Advisory Board;
California Wine Institute; Florida Department of Citrus;
Fresh Bartlett Promotion Advisory Board; Glenn Embree; Halibut Association of North America;
Idaho Oregon Sweet Spanish Onion Promotion Committee; The McIlhenny Company (Tabasco);
National Fisheries Institute; Nectarine Administrative Committee;
The Quaker Oats Company; South African Rock Lobster Association;
Spanish Green Olive Commission; Washington State Apple Commission; Wheat Flour Institute

FOREWORD

How thirteen colonies became fifty states is a story that never fails to fascinate Americans. It unfolds like a drama, with scenes changing from frost-bitten New England to the Mid-Atlantic seaboard, down through the South, across the Midwest, Southwest, and West, and reaches its climax with the entry of Alaska and Hawaii.

As the settings changed, so did the ways of the people. The newcomers brought their old-world cooking styles with them, but as they moved, their recipes were adapted to suit the food at hand. The new land actually shaped the people as much as they shaped it.

The European arrivals found their new home already occupied by people with cooking methods different from their own. From the Indians and Mexicans they acquired new ways that eased their assimilation into the New World.

Those early Americans felt that they had a "manifest destiny" to claim the continent. Given a twentieth-century perspective, their push westward is taken for granted. But from their standpoint it must have seemed an enormous challenge, considering the difficulty of meeting everyday needs in unfamiliar surroundings.

Today's cook has it far easier. The land has been won, and so has the battle with Nature for food. The supermarket offers everything we need, often in a form ready to eat with no further effort.

But since less time is needed to find food, more is available to cook it in interesting ways. One of the techniques of creative cooks is to borrow from the culinary heritage of early America.

Another is to make the acquaintance of recipes from other regions. Today, space and time are no longer obstacles; modern travel accommodations make it possible to go from coast to coast—or to Hawaii—in just hours. Such mobility has introduced Americans to the foods of other states, and this has helped them to vary daily menus when back home. And modern transportation carries the specialty foods from one state to all the rest, making regional recipes easy to duplicate, given the appropriate recipes.

Realizing the need to update heirloom "receipts" into today's language and for use with today's food products, the CULINARY ARTS INSTITUTE has tested and compiled those most representative of the various regions. The biggest challenge to the editors was the selection and placement of the recipes. Some dishes, such as apple pie, belong as much to one state as another. In such cases, the recipe was placed to give balance, so that the chapter for each state provides the makings for a complete menu. To find a specific dish, look in the index.

The CULINARY ARTS INSTITUTE has discriminated carefully among possible recipes in making the selections for each state. Entries were selected to give as much variety as possible. Other recipes were well qualified to be included, but space limited the selection.

Since 1936, the CULINARY ARTS INSTITUTE has supplied American cooks with some of their best-known and most widely used cookbooks and booklets. CULINARY ARTS INSTITUTE recipes have all been prepared in its test kitchen and approved by a taste panel before publication.

Not only will *The Fifty States Cookbook* provide you with a broader perspective of American cooking; you will also find it a source of greater variety and enjoyment at mealtime.

CONTENTS

Connecticut, third smallest state in the United States, is also a favorite vacationland of contrasting beauty and great diversity. It is famous for both its picturesque rural towns and its huge urban centers. Most of its people live and work within the boundaries of the state, but there are many who commute miles each day into the metropolitan environs of New York City. Thus, today, the traditional New England modes of eating and living are being combined with those of a vast eastern megalopolis. For example, typical New England clam chowder never contains tomatoes. But in Connecticut, this chowder is prepared with tomatoes and is referred to as "Manhattan" clam chowder.

The first white settlers arrived in Connecticut in 1633 from the Netherlands. They built a small fort near Hartford, today's capital, but were never considered a permanent community. It was the English colonists from Massachusetts, led by Thomas Hooker, Roger Ludlow, and John Haynes in the 1600s, who, wanting to flee from the rigid authoritarianism of their former communities, built permanent homes along the Connecticut River. These hearty people brought their thrifty habits of food production and preparation with them. All early New Englanders were forced to use what the land and waters provided for them. Corn, beans, squash, and pumpkins came from their harvest, myriad seafoods from their coastal waters, and meat and poultry from their forests filled with wild game. Although typical New England puddings, stews, and pies are abundant in the state, Connecticut does have good reason to boast of a few indigenous dishes and variations of the so-called "traditional." Pumpkins of all shapes and sizes are made into the most delicious pies and moist brown breads. Pumpkin bread was supposedly a favorite among the Revolutionary War heroes two hundred years ago.

Connecticut has often been referred to as the "Nutmeg State." However, even though Connecticut homemakers have always used nutmeg and other spices liberally in their cooking, the nickname originated from the days when shrewd Yankee peddlers sold wooden nutmegs in place of the scarce and valuable real thing, and not from the numerous spice-laden local recipes.

A very special election-day cake which originated in Hartford is a traditional New England favorite. Town meeting and election days were always great events, and people would gather for parties of punch and cake to celebrate victory or defeat. This special cake is prepared from flour, yeast, spices, nuts, and citron and is usually served with thick, rich cream, often whipped.

Onions were grown by the early settlers and some were even exported to the West Indies for profit. But these succulent vegetables also found their way into many a hearty midday stew or chowder. A regional stew of beef, bacon fat, onions, potatoes, and carrots, flavored with fresh garden-grown Con-necticut herbs, is especially delicious when served over rosemary-flavored biscuits.

The mighty Connecticut River has always been a fisherman's haven. Broiled river shad is a local specialty. Oysters, flounders, lobsters, and clams are found near Long Island Sound. Clambakes and oyster roasts are popular pastimes. Seafood fanciers love to visit Mystic Seaport and Marine Museum, a restored whaling village in Mystic, Connecticut. It was built to recall the state's seafaring traditions of the 1800s.

New England and Connecticut cookery traditions are world famous. The first American printed cookbook was written by Amelia Simmons and published in Hartford in 1796. The Shaker establishment at Enfield is said to have distributed the first commercial seed in the United States. Their simple tastes in food meshed well with spartan Yankee fare. One of their successful recipes still with us today is Shaker Braised Steak, a delectable combination of vegetables, lemon juice, ketchup, and ordinary beef round steak.

Beef à la Mode

1½ pounds beef for stew, cubed
½ cup flour
1½ teaspoons salt
¼ teaspoon pepper
3 tablespoons bacon fat
4 carrots, pared and sliced
1 large onion, sliced
6 potatoes, pared and quartered
1 can (29 ounces) tomatoes, drained (reserve juice)
Herb mixture (1 tablespoon each basil, chervil, marjoram, and savory)
Rosemary Biscuits

1. Coat meat cubes with a mixture of flour, salt, and pepper, reserving remaining flour mixture.
2. Brown cubes in bacon fat.
3. Put meat into a deep casserole. Add carrots, onion, potatoes, and drained tomatoes.
4. Stir remaining seasoned flour into fat left in skillet. When mixture bubbles, gradually add reserved tomato juice, stirring constantly. Cook until slightly thickened.
5. Tie herb mixture in cheesecloth and add to casserole. Pour thickened liquid over meat and vegetables; add enough water to almost cover vegetables. Cover.
6. Bake at 325°F 3½ to 4 hours.
7. Serve over Rosemary Biscuits.

6 servings

Rosemary Biscuits: Prepare Baking Powder Biscuits (page 31), adding **1 teaspoon crushed rosemary** with the dry ingredients.

Shaker Braised Steak

3 **pounds beef round steak**
2 **tablespoons flour**
2 **tablespoons butter**
1 **teaspoon salt**
¼ **teaspoon pepper**
1 **stalk celery, chopped**
1 **carrot, finely chopped**
½ **green pepper, finely chopped**
2 **medium onions, finely chopped**
  Juice of ½ lemon
½ **cup ketchup**

1. Coat meat with flour.
2. Sauté in heated butter until well browned on both sides. Season with salt and pepper. Add chopped vegetables, lemon juice, and ketchup.
3. Cover tightly and simmer gently 2 to 2½ hours, or until steak is tender when tested with a fork.

About 6 servings

Baked Steak with Oyster Filling

1 **beef round steak (2 pounds), cut ½ inch thick**
¼ **teaspoon salt**
¼ **teaspoon paprika**
3 **tablespoons flour**
¼ **cup water**
  Oyster Filling
6 **potatoes, pared and cubed (optional)**
6 **onions, chopped (optional)**
6 **carrots, pared and sliced (optional)**

1. Pound steak and sprinkle with seasonings; cut in half. Put 1 steak into a shallow 3-quart baking pan, cover with filling, and top with remaining steak. Sprinkle with flour. Add water and cover.
2. Bake at 350°F 1¼ hours. Baste occasionally, adding more water as necessary.
3. If desired, after the first half hour add potatoes, onions, and carrots to the baking pan to cook with the meat.

6 servings

Oyster Filling: Mix **1 cup chopped oysters, 2 cups soft bread crumbs, 1 tablespoon minced parsley, ¼ teaspoon celery seed, ¼ teaspoon minced onion,** and **¼ cup melted butter.** Use as directed.

Broiled Connecticut River Shad

1 **shad (3 to 4 pounds)**
  Melted butter
  Salt and pepper
  Parsley
¼ **cup butter**
1 **tablespoon lemon juice**

1. Have shad cleaned and split. Place skin side down on an oiled and preheated plank or broiler-proof platter. Brush with melted butter and sprinkle with salt and pepper.
2. Broil until tender, 15 to 20 minutes, depending upon size and thickness of fish. Remove to a serving platter and garnish with parsley.
3. Beat butter until softened; add lemon juice gradually, creaming until blended. Spread over fish. Serve at once.

6 to 8 servings

Stuffed Clams

24 littleneck clams
3 fresh mushrooms, chopped fine
2 slices bacon, fried and finely crumbled
1 teaspoon minced parsley
   Salt and pepper
   Bread crumbs
   Butter or margarine

1. Cover bottom of a shallow baking pan with **rock salt**.
2. Scrub clams well and place in rock salt to hold clams in place and prevent liquor from running out when clams open.
3. Set in a 400°F oven until clams begin to open.
4. Remove from oven. Remove clams from shells; save liquor. Chop clams and combine with the clam liquor, mushrooms, bacon, parsley, salt, and pepper. Add enough bread crumbs to thicken, so that the mixture will hold its shape in shells; mix thoroughly.
5. Fill the clam shells. Sprinkle with bread crumbs and dot with butter.
6. Bake at 350°F about 12 minutes, or until brown on top.

4 servings

Oysters Baked in Shells

24 large oysters and shells
1 egg
½ teaspoon salt
⅛ teaspoon pepper
1 tablespoon cold water
1 cup bread crumbs
   Butter

1. Scrub the shells carefully to remove any sand or dirt.
2. Beat egg with salt, pepper, and water.
3. Dip oysters into the egg mixture, then into the crumbs. Place oysters back in shells; dot with butter.
4. Bake at 450°F 10 minutes.

4 servings

New England Baked Pumpkin

1 pumpkin or acorn squash (about 2 pounds)
⅓ cup butter, melted
½ cup lightly packed brown sugar
1½ tablespoons chopped crystallized ginger
1 teaspoon cinnamon
¼ teaspoon salt

1. Cut pumpkin in quarters; remove seeds. Place pumpkin pieces in a greased shallow baking pan.
2. Combine remaining ingredients and spoon onto pumpkin.
3. Bake at 350°F about 1 hour, or until tender; baste occasionally during baking.

4 servings

Pumpkin Vegetable Skillet

4 cups pared diced
    pumpkin or 4 sweet
    potatoes, pared and
    diced
¼ cup bacon drippings
½ cup onion slices
1 clove garlic, minced
2 cups cut green beans
1 cup whole kernel corn
1 cup chopped tomatoes
½ cup chopped green
    pepper
1 teaspoon salt
½ teaspoon chili powder
¼ teaspoon pepper
½ cup chicken broth

1. Cook pumpkin in bacon drippings 5 minutes.
2. Add remaining ingredients; mix well. Cook covered over low heat 40 to 45 minutes, or until vegetables are tender.

6 servings

Pumpkin Bread

1 cup warm water
¾ cup sugar
1 package active dry yeast
3 tablespoons oil
2 teaspoons salt
1 cup canned pumpkin
½ cup instant nonfat dry
    milk
5 cups all-purpose flour
    (about)

1. Put water, sugar, and yeast into a large bowl; stir until sugar and a yeast are dissolved. Let stand 5 minutes.
2. Add oil, salt, pumpkin, and dry milk; beat well.
3. Gradually beat in enough flour to make a soft dough. Knead on a lightly floured surface until dough is smooth and elastic. Put into a greased bowl, cover, and let rise until double in bulk (about 1½ hours).
4. Punch down dough, turn over in bowl, cover, and let rise again until double in bulk (about 45 minutes).
5. Punch dough down and shape into two loaves. Put loaves into 2 greased 8×4×3-inch loaf pans. Cover; let rise until double in bulk (about 45 minutes).
6. Bake at 400°F 25 to 30 minutes.

2 loaves

Hasty Pudding

1 cup cornmeal
1½ teaspoons salt
½ cup cold water
2½ cups boiling water

1. Make a paste of the cornmeal, salt, and cold water, stirring until there are no lumps, and pour gradually into the boiling water, stirring constantly. Cook and stir until very thick.
2. Put into a double boiler, cover, and cook 30 minutes, stirring occasionally.
3. Serve hot with **sugar** and **milk,** or with plenty of **butter,** or as desired.

6 servings

Election Day Yeast Cake

½ cup milk
2 packages active dry
    yeast
½ cup warm water
1½ cups sifted all-purpose
    flour
1¾ cups sifted all-purpose
    flour
1 teaspoon salt
1½ teaspoons cinnamon
½ teaspoon mace
½ teaspoon nutmeg
¼ teaspoon cloves
½ cup butter
¾ cup sugar
3 eggs, well beaten
1 cup pecans, chopped
½ cup chopped candied
    citron

1. Scald milk and cool to lukewarm.
2. Meanwhile, soften yeast in warm water in a bowl; set aside.
3. Add the lukewarm milk to softened yeast. Add 1½ cups flour gradually, beating well after each addition. Beat until mixture is smooth. Cover bowl with waxed paper and a clean towel and let rise in a warm place until very light and bubbly (about 45 minutes).
4. Meanwhile, blend remaining flour, salt, and spices.
5. Beat butter until softened. Add sugar gradually, creaming until fluffy after each addition. Add eggs in thirds, beating thoroughly after each addition.
6. Blend in yeast mixture. Gradually add dry ingredients, beating until smooth after addition. Add pecans and citron and mix well. Turn mixture into a greased (bottom only) 9-inch tube pan.
7. Cover with waxed paper and towel and let rise in a warm place until pan is almost full (about 2 hours).
8. Bake at 350°F 50 to 55 minutes. Remove from oven to wire rack and cool 10 minutes in pan. Cut around tube with paring knife to loosen cake. Loosen sides with spatula; invert on rack and lift off pan. Cool completely before slicing.

One 9-inch tube cake

Connecticut Crullers

2 tablespoons butter or
    other shortening
1 cup sugar
2 eggs, well beaten
4 cups sifted all-purpose
    flour
3½ teaspoons baking
    powder
½ teaspoon grated nutmeg
½ teaspoon salt
1 cup cream
    Fat for deep frying
      heated to 360°F
    Confectioners' sugar

1. Cream butter and sugar until thoroughly mixed. Add eggs and beat well.
2. Sift dry ingredients together and add alternately with cream to creamed mixture, mixing thoroughly.
3. Put dough on a well-floured surface and pat lightly until just thick enough to cut in thin strips ½ inch wide. Bring edges together to form a circle, leaving a hole in center, and press together.
4. Fry in hot fat until brown. Drain on absorbent paper. Dust with confectioners' sugar.

2 dozen crullers

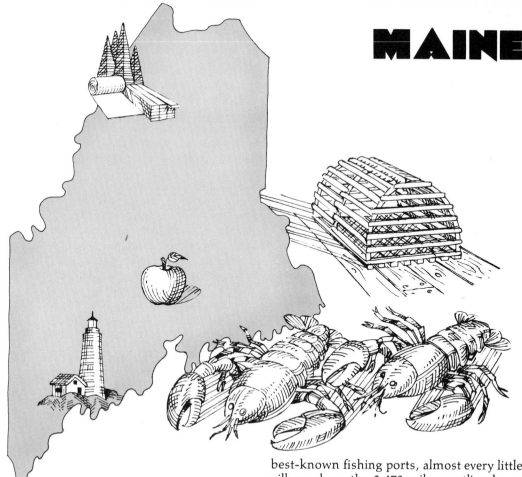

Maine, the "Pine Tree State," with its glorious crystal-clear lakes, towering trees, and rugged natural coastline, is the eastern-most state in the United States. At one time most of its land was covered with virgin white pine. Even today forests cover 90 percent of the state. The production of lumber and paper is the leading industry; however, farming and fishing are also important. Most of the fertile farmland is located in the New England upland, a plateau covering the central and eastern part of the state. The White Mountain region in the west rises over five thousand feet and is filled with blue lakes, gorges, and spectacular scenery. The coastal lowlands near the Atlantic are in the southwestern section. Hundreds of islands are located in Maine's many bays and inlets.

Although Portland and Rockland are the best-known fishing ports, almost every little village along the 3,478 mile coastline has a small fleet of fishing boats. And the proud Maine fishermen will not let you forget that their lobster catch, along with clams, cod, pollack, scallops, flounder, and sardines, ranks among the nation's biggest. Down Easterners, as the people of Maine are called (early New Englanders used "down" for "north"), will tell you to come to Maine if you want real lobster. You will find lobster boiled, lobster broiled, lobster in salads, and lobster in soups. There are endless recipes for this local specialty, and they are all superb. Simplicity is the key to most of these dishes, for the people of Maine say that lobster is best when allowed to give you its own delicate flavor. Clams are also popular in the state, and a real treat is a regional cream of clam soup prepared very simply with shelled clams, milk, butter, flour, and seasonings.

English explorers arrived in Maine before the Pilgrims made it to Plymouth, but the

MAINE

first permanent English settlers built homes there in the middle 1620s. For almost a century they were subjected to the French and Indian Wars and were forced to adopt prudent and innovative methods of survival. This rugged pioneer background, combined with a cold and moist climate, helped many early Maine homemakers develop habits of thrift and ingenuity in managing their colonial kitchens. Foods from the forests were utilized, including the extraordinary wild roots and berries. Strawberries, blueberries, and raspberries are still abundant in Maine today and find their way into numerous delectable breads and desserts.

Potatoes are one of Maine's most important crops. Acadians from the eastern province of Canada brought the first potatoes to Aroostook County in the central plateau long before Maine became a state. Today, only Idaho grows more potatoes than Maine. Meat or fish and potatoes are the mainstay of the Down Easterners' diet. Potatoes, such as the Katahdins that come from north central Maine, are popular for thickening the typical New England stews and chowders. These regional soups are always the thick, meal-in-one varieties. Potato doughnuts and rolls, prepared from fresh or leftover mashed potatoes, are other Yankee-inspired ways of using this staple vegetable.

Delicious and McIntosh apples, Maine's chief fruit crop, are grown in the southern counties. New Englanders use apples in a variety of both main dish and dessert recipes. Apple Betty, prepared from leftover bread crumbs, brown sugar, and tart apples, is a good example of the conservative creativity of the region.

Livestock and poultry are also important to Maine's economy. Broilers are raised throughout the farm regions of the state. A favorite dish for many Down Easterners is fried chicken with a crispy crust.

Molasses and ginger, kitchen staples of old New England, are also used extensively in local cookery. Gingersnaps, gingerbreads, and pots of baked beans greet hungry families at many a Maine meal.

Grilled Lobster

1 live lobster (about 1½
  pounds)
Tabasco Butter

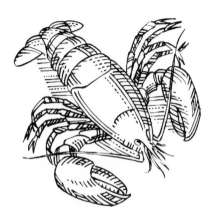

1. Purchase a lobster for each serving. Live lobsters may be killed and dressed for cooking at the market. If prepared at home, place the lobster on a cutting board with back or smooth shell up. Hold a towel firmly over the head and claws. Kill by quickly inserting the point of a sharp heavy knife into the center of the small cross showing on the back of the head. Without removing knife, quickly bear down heavily, cutting through entire length of the body and tail. Split the halves apart and remove the stomach, a small sac which lies in the head, and the spongy lungs which lie between meat and shell. Also remove the dark intestinal line running through the center of the body. Crack large claws with a nutcracker or mallet.

2. Brush meat with Tabasco Butter. Place shell side down on grill about 5 inches from coals. Grill about 20 minutes, or until shell is browned. Baste frequently with butter. Serve in shell with remaining butter.

Tabasco Butter: Melt ½ **cup butter** and stir in ½ **teaspoon Tabasco** and **1 tablespoon lime juice.**

Grilled Lobster, 16